# Contents

KW-495-798

# 1 Working with text: Going on holiday

**By the end of this unit you will:**

→ know more about the keyboard

→ know how to delete words and add full stops

→ know how to add text and use line breaks

→ know how to change the colour of a word.

**In this unit you are going to make a travel brochure.**

We can use words to persuade people to do things, such as go on holiday to a favourite place.

Using a computer can help us improve our writing and make sure we give all the right information. You are going to learn more about ways of making your words look special.

## Activity | Where would you like to go?

Where would you like to travel to? Make a list of all the places. Draw or cut out pictures from brochures of some of the places.

**brochure** **delete** **edit** **keyboard** **line break**

### Talk about...

Do you have any special places? Where are they? Why are they special?

### Fascinating fact

Niagara Falls is one of the top five most visited places on earth.

5

## You will learn:

→ to find your way around the keyboard
→ how to use the backspace key and space bar.

### The QWERTY keyboard

Do you remember where the letters are on the **keyboard**?

Do you remember where the numbers are on the keyboard?

This type of keyboard is called a QWERTY keyboard – can you work out why?

**1** This is the 'Caps Lock' key. Do you remember what it does?

**2** This is the backspace key. You can use it to **delete** text.

**3** This is the space bar. It makes gaps between words.

### How to use the space bar

Find the space bar on your keyboard.

Press it quickly.

What happens to the cursor?

Now press it for a count of 1, 2, 3, 4, 5.

What happens to the cursor?

Remember, the cursor is the pointer.

## Activity  Opening and saving a file

**1** Open a new file.

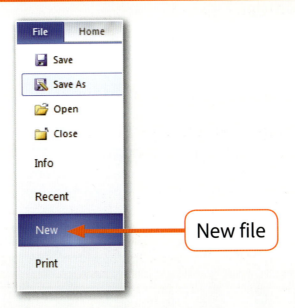

New file

**2** Look at the words your teacher has given you. These are words you could use in your travel **brochure**.

**3** Type the first word onto your page and press the space bar.

**4** Do this for all the words.

**5** Save your file.

**1** Remember to name your file.

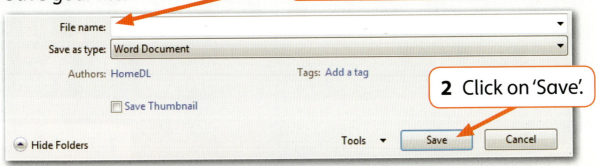

**2** Click on 'Save'.

**Talk about...**
Think about which words would be good for your travel brochure.

 **If you have time...**
Explain to each other what the travel words you have found mean.

## You will learn:

→ how to delete words
→ how to use full stops.

When we write, we use an eraser to remove a word.

When we type, we can delete a word to remove it. We can do this using the backspace key.

A full stop shows us it is the end of a sentence.

**1** The backspace key

**2** The full stop key

### How to delete a word

Click on the *end* of the word you want to delete.

Press the backspace key until the word has gone.

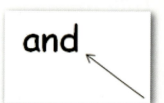

## Activity  Deleting a word

 Open the document your teacher has given you.

Read the first line and find the word 'and'. Click the end of the word.

Press the backspace key until the word 'and' has gone.

Press the full stop key once to put in a full stop after the word 'park'.

## Talk about...
You have made a sentence. What do you need to do to the first letter of the next word? How do you do this?

## Activity  Using 'Caps Lock'

Use the 'Caps Lock' key to start the next sentence with an upper-case letter.

Save your file.

 **If you have time...**
Look through the rest of the writing to see if there are other places you could delete 'and' and make sentences.

## Talk about...
Do you like the piece of writing? What would you change for your brochure?

## You will learn:

➜ how to add text to your page.

A travel brochure tells you information about a holiday or place. What sorts of information would you like to know?

Is it warm or... cold?

Are there fun things to do?

What sort of food is there?

How can I get there? By car? In an aeroplane? On a bus?

## How to choose the right words

When we are trying to make a place sound exciting to someone else, we need to choose our words carefully.

Instead of saying the food is 'nice', it makes it more exciting to say the food is 'delicious'.

## Activity  Making your writing sound exciting

Work with a partner.

Open a new file.

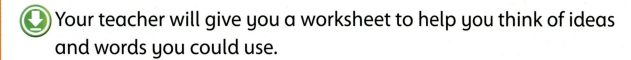 Your teacher will give you a worksheet to help you think of ideas and words you could use.

Type two sentences.

Remember: each sentence should start with an upper case letter and end with a full stop. Put a space between each word.

Think about the sorts of words to use.

How can you make the place sound interesting and exciting?

### Talk about...
Your teacher will share with the class some of the sentences you have written.

Which words work well?

### If you have time...
Write some more sentences. Make your words sound tempting and interesting.

## You will learn:

➜ how to use line breaks.

Look at this text.

```
passport    toothbrush    sunglasses
towel    toothpaste    pyjamas
book    games    sandals    hat
T-shirt    coat    socks
```

**Talk about…**
How could we make this list easier to read and tick off?

We can use the 'Enter' key at the end of each word to start a new line. This makes an easy-to-read list, like this:

```
passport

toothbrush

sunglasses

towel

…
```

You can use the **line break** to make line spaces between your sentences, too.

## How to make a line break

**1** Find the 'Enter' key on the keyboard.

This is the 'Enter' key, sometimes called the 'Return' key.

**2** Move your cursor to where you want to make a line break in your text on the screen.

Move the cursor to here.

passport toothbrush sunglasses towel toothpaste pyjamas book games sandals hat t-shirt coat socks

**3** Click on the mouse and press the 'Enter' key on the keyboard.

## Activity Making line breaks

Open your saved file.

Choose a place in your writing to try out a line break. Now continue to write the text for your travel brochure.

Save your file.

### If you have time…

Write a travel poem on screen. Use the 'Enter' key at the end of each line.

## You will learn:

→ how to change the colour of the text.

We can change the colour of text to make it look more interesting.

Colours can have meaning.

Blue text might be chosen to show something is calm and peaceful.

Red text is often used to show danger.

## How to type a word in a different colour

1 Highlight the word you would like to change.

2 Look at the toolbar.

3 Click the font colour letter 'A'?

4 Choose and click on a colour you like. What happens to the word?

2 Toolbar

3 Font colour

4 Colours

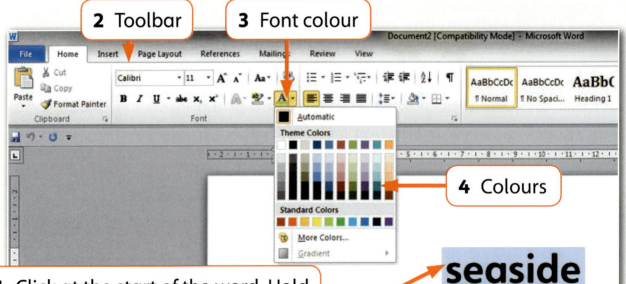

1 Click at the start of the word. Hold down the mouse button. Drag along the word to highlight it.

seaside

## Activity  Making different coloured words

Open your saved file.

Type some words in a different colour. The colour could match the place you are writing about.

What does it look like?

Save your file.

This is a forest

## Talk about...
Which colours look good on the screen?

## If you have time...
There are many more colours you can try. Find out how to do this.

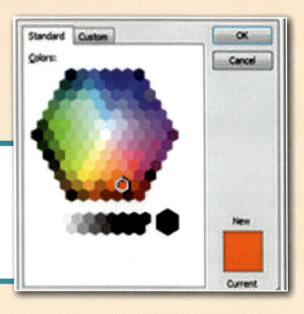

## You will learn:

→ how to **edit** your work to make it better.

This is a page from a travel company brochure. It gives the reader information and makes them want to go on the holiday.

**Talk about...**
What features of the brochure do you like? Can you see any features you have learned how to use in this unit?

## How to complete your writing

Open your saved file.

Read through your sentences carefully. If you see anything that looks wrong, delete it and type it again. This is called editing.

Save the file.

Now for a holiday filled
un and adventure. We
exciting programmes and
ties for 4 to 10 year olds.

## Activity  Editing

Edit your writing. Use this checklist to help you.

→ Does each sentence start with an upper case letter?

→ Does each sentence end with a full stop?

→ Is there a space between each word?

→ Have you used colour to make the words look interesting?

→ Are there line breaks to help the reader?

→ Have you used words that make your place sound tempting to the reader?

→ Save your file.

## If you have time...

Think about what you might have on the cover of your brochure.

# What you have learned about working with text

You have learned about some new keys on the keyboard, how to delete words, make line breaks and type words in different colours and how to edit.

The activities on this page will let you see how much you have learned.

**1** What do these words mean?

- delete

_____

_____

- line break

_____

_____

- edit

_____

_____

**2** How can you make your words look special?

_____

_____

_____

18

© Oxford University Press 2015

## Activity  Knowing the keyboard

Show your teacher where these keys are on the keyboard.

→ Caps Lock

→ space bar

→ full stop

→ Enter

→ backspace

© Oxford University Press 2015

# 2 Multimedia: Holiday images

**By the end of this unit you will:**

➔ know how to find and choose pictures to go with your words

➔ know how to change pictures to make them look interesting

➔ learn to put pictures and words together in one document

➔ know what the parts of a page are.

**In this unit you are going to make a poster for your favourite place.**

Pictures can help people understand what we write about. We can use the computer to put words and pictures together on a page.

In this unit you are going to learn more about ways of putting words and pictures together.

Clip Art   template   document   effects   page elements   Word Art

**Activity** — Choosing words and pictures

What words and pictures would you like to put on a poster about your favourite place?

**Talk about...**

What posters have you seen at school? And at home? And outdoors? Can you describe them?

**Fascinating fact**

All the posters you see at the shops and in the cinema are designed using computers. And you can make one too!

## You will learn:

➜ how to find and choose pictures for your work
➜ how to put pictures in your work and make them fit.

Some programs have lots of pictures you can choose to put in your work. These pictures are called **Clip Art**.

**Activity** | **Finding and adding Clip Art pictures**

⬇ Open the **template** in *Microsoft Word*. Your teacher will show you where to find the file.

Find a Clip Art picture that is right for each box in the template.

Insert the picture in the right place.

If the picture is too big or too small, resize it so that it fits.

22

# How to find Clip Art and add it to your document

Click on the place where you want to put your picture.

**2** This is where you can search for images using a word, such as 'transport'.

**1** Click the Clip Art icon here under the Insert tab.

**4** Drag the handles at the corners to make the picture smaller or bigger.

**3** When you have found the picture you want you can use 'Insert' to put it in your document.

## Talk about...

Are some search words better than others? Is there a better word you could use instead of 'place'?

## If you have time...

⬇ Write down the story that your pictures tell.

Where are you going?

Who with?

How will you travel there?

What will you do?

## You will learn:

➜ how to put words and pictures together in one document

➜ how to move pictures and change their size so that they fit together well with your text.

Word-processing programs let you put words and pictures together. There are many ways you can put words and pictures together to make your work look good.

### Talk about...

What are the things you must think about when you put images and text together?

# How to put a picture together with text

You can use the 'Wrap Text' menu to select how you want the text to surround the picture.

You can move your picture by clicking and dragging it to a new place.

Try turning your picture.

Can you remember how to make a picture bigger or smaller?

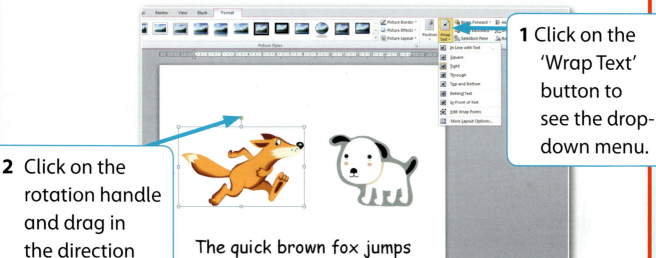

**1** Click on the 'Wrap Text' button to see the drop-down menu.

**2** Click on the rotation handle and drag in the direction you want your picture to turn.

## Activity — Adding pictures to text

Open the template in *Microsoft Word*. Move the pictures onto the text. Watch how the text changes when you move the pictures over them.

Try resizing, moving and rotating the images.

Find the best way of putting the images and text together to make a nice **document**.

## You will learn:

→ how to add a border to your picture
→ how to add effects to your picture.

Adding effects to a picture means changing the colour or shape of the picture.

Many programs let you change the way your pictures look. You can add borders and **effects** to get just the look you want.

A border is a design which surrounds a picture.

## How to add borders

In *Microsoft Word* you can add borders in two ways.

**1.** You can choose a style of border in 'Picture Styles'.

**2.** You can choose your border's type of line and its colour in 'Picture Border'.

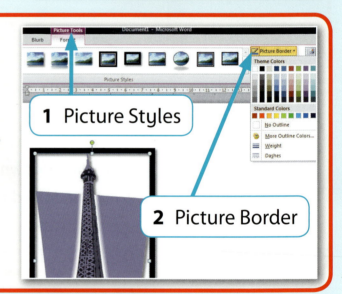

**1** Picture Styles

**2** Picture Border

## Activity | Border and colour

⬇ Open the template in *Microsoft Word*.

→ Use 'Picture Styles' and 'Picture Border' to add your favourite border to the poster.

→ Use the 'Color' menu to change the colour of the hats.

→ Save your work.

# How to add effects

You can add lots of different effects to your picture.

**1** Use the 'Color' menu to change the colour of your picture.

**2** Move the cursor over each effect to see how it changes the picture.

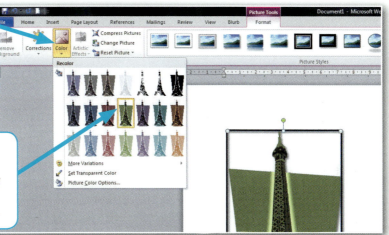

**3** Use the 'Picture Effects' menu to add shadow, make glowing outlines, etc.

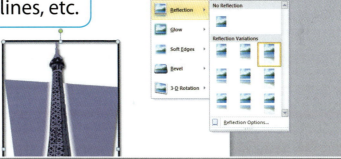

**4** You can use 'Artistic Effects'. Click here to make the picture look like a pencil drawing.

## You will learn:

➔ how to add text in boxes and other shapes
➔ how to put text boxes and shapes together with pictures.

Putting text in boxes means you can put your text anywhere on the page.

### How to add a text box...

In *Microsoft Word* you can choose different kinds of boxes for text.

Type your text into this box.

This is my text box!

Use the mouse pointer to move and resize the box.

### ...or a shape...

*Microsoft Word* also lets you add text in shapes to make your document more exciting.

**1** Choose a shape from the 'Shapes' menu.

**3** Type here.

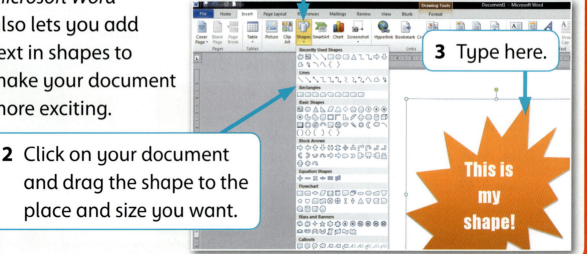

This is my shape!

**2** Click on your document and drag the shape to the place and size you want.

## ...and change the way they look

You can change the way text boxes and shapes look by changing settings on the 'Shape Styles' menus – 'Shape Fill', 'Shape Outline' and 'Shape Effects'. Click the mouse to make the change.

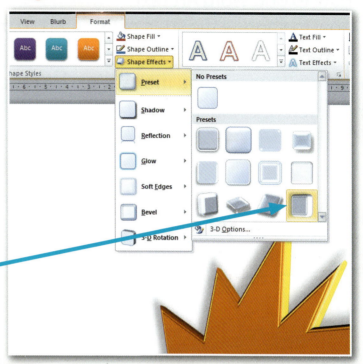

Move the cursor over the change to see the effect.

## Activity | Adding text boxes

 Open the template in *Microsoft Word*.

Find the right shapes and add them to the template. Add some text and change the size of the shape to make it fit. Now move the shapes into the best position.

## Talk about...

Why might shapes with words in them be useful? Which shapes work best with words in them? Why?

## If you have time...

Change the font of your text in each shape. Change the background colour to match the picture.

## You will learn:

→ how to add Word Art text

→ how to change the style of Word Art to make titles.

*Microsoft Word* lets you make **Word Art** to give text different shapes and different colours.

### How to add Word Art...

Word Art is good for titles or headings on your document.

Move the Word Art box by dragging it. You can resize it too.

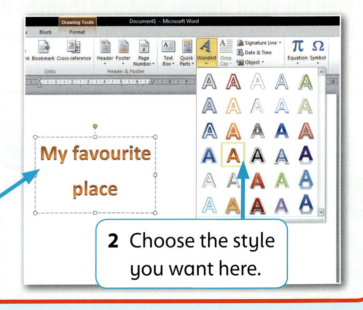

**1** Type your text in the Word Art box.

**2** Choose the style you want here.

# ...and change the way it looks

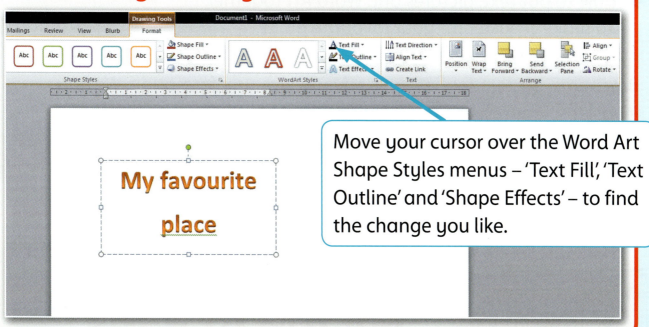

Move your cursor over the Word Art Shape Styles menus – 'Text Fill', 'Text Outline' and 'Shape Effects' – to find the change you like.

## Activity | Using Word Art

Open a new document in *Microsoft Word*.

Create three Word Art boxes, each with your name in it. Make sure all the Word Art boxes fit on the page.

In the first Word Art, change the text fill colour to your favourite colour.

In the second Word Art, add an outline to your text.

In the third Word Art, add a text effect from the menu.

## Talk about...

What do we have to be careful about when using Word Art?

## If you have time...

Give each Word Art in the activity a different font. Which is your favourite?

## You will learn:

➜ how to put text, pictures and Word Art together to make a poster for your favourite place.

Brochures, posters, leaflets and adverts give us information. We find it easier to understand information when it is properly organised.

This poster about Paris has many different parts. They are called **page elements**.

### How to plan your page

**1 Title.** In a newspaper or magazine this is called a 'headline'. It should be large and easy to read. It should explain what the page is about.

**2 Body text.** This is the main part of the page.

**3 Pull quote.** This is a text box or shape that lets you say the really important things.

**4 Image.** The picture should relate to the body text.

**5 Caption.** This explains what your image is about.

My trip to Paris

I want to go to Paris with my mum, dad and brother.

Paris is the capital city of France!

We will go to Disney. I won't eat snails. I prefer cakes.

The Eiffel Tower is a famous building in Paris.

**Explore Paris**
**Book your holiday now!**

Come and explore the wonderful city of Paris. Lots of surprises are in store for you! Visit the magnificent Eiffel Tower. Go museum-hopping. Play in the wonderful amusement park and take back with you beautiful memories. Book Soon!

'The Eiffel Tower' is the tallest structure in Paris.

## Activity — Making a poster

 Open a new document in *Microsoft Word* and make a poster of your favourite place.

→ Make a title using Word Art.

→ Add a text box for the body text.

→ Find and add a Clip Art image.

▲ An example of a brochure page showing different elements

**Talk about...**
What place did you choose and why?

### If you have time...

Make a pull quote. Add a shape to your page and type into it.

Add a caption to your image. Make a text box that fits below your image. Type in some text that describes your image.

# What you have learned about multimedia

You have learned how to find and choose pictures to go with your words, how to change pictures, how to put pictures and words together and what the parts of a page are.

The activities on this page will let you see how much you have learned.

1 What do these words mean?

- Clip Art

_____

_____

- template

_____

_____

- effects

_____

_____

2 How can you make your words look special at the top of a poster?

_____

_____

34

© Oxford University Press 2015

## Activity | Making a poster

Make a poster about your school. Include these page elements:

➜ a title

➜ a text box

➜ a picture

➜ a caption.

Write down the name of each element next to it on your poster.

35

© Oxford University Press 2015

# 3 The internet: Learning with the internet

**By the end of this unit you will:**

→ know how to use a search engine to find information online

→ know how to use bookmarks or favourites

→ know how to add a bookmark to a bookmark website

→ understand about tagging

→ know how to find links on a bookmark website

→ understand how to check websites.

**In this unit you are going to make a bookmark list about minibeasts.**

There is a lot of information on the **internet**. You can find many websites that could be useful or interesting. We can use **bookmarks**, **favourites** and libraries to store website addresses we might want to use another time.

**Talk about...**
Do you use a bookmark when you read a book? What do you think an online bookmark might be? Why could it be useful?

## Activity | Making a bookmark

Make a bookmark in the shape of a caterpillar.

bookmark
browser         tag
search engine
internet     favourite
URL

## Fascinating fact

Honey bees talk to each other by dancing. How do we communicate?

37

## You will learn:

→ how to use a search engine to find information online.

How would you find a book on butterflies in this library?

The internet is like an enormous online library, with websites instead of books. We use **search engines** to help us find the websites we need.

Search engines send software robots called 'spiders' to visit websites. For each visit, the spider makes a list of words. The words become part of a big list. When we type a key word into a search engine, we are searching the big list.

# How to use a search engine

Here are some different search engines. To search, type your key word into the space and press the enter key.

## Activity    Finding out about butterflies

Type 'butterfly' into a search engine.

Click on the first website and explore it.

## Talk about…

What did you find out about butterflies? Was it easy to find information? What did you like about the site?

 **If you have time…**

Write down the **URL** of the website you have found. A URL is the name of the file on the internet.

# 3.2 | Bookmarks and favourites

## You will learn:

➔ how to use bookmarks or favourites.

A bookmark is a way of remembering a place in a book.

Online bookmarks are a way of remembering a place on the internet.

**Browsers** help us to look at websites on the internet. Some browsers call bookmarks favourites.

### How to add a favourite

Internet Explorer uses favourites. Open Internet Explorer and go to a website you would like to add.

Most browsers have a star icon to show where to add a bookmark, just like this one.

**2** Click 'Add to favourites'. A dialogue box will open. A dialogue box is a window that opens to let you carry out a task.

**1** Click the star in the top right-hand corner of the screen.

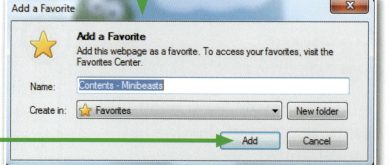

**3** Click 'Add'.

## Activity  Adding a bookmark or a favourite

Look at the website about beetles, shown on your screen. Add a bookmark of the website to your computer.

## Talk about...

What did you like about the website on beetles?

What did you not like?

Did you believe the information you found?

Did you find information easily?

## If you have time...

Create a folder for your favourites called 'Minibeasts'.

Clue: find the 'New folder' button in the dialogue box if you are using Internet Explorer.

## You will learn:

→ how to add a bookmark to a bookmarking website.

When you add a bookmark to your browser, it means you can find the website when you come back to your computer.

But what if you wanted to find your link when you were working on a computer at home? Or another place altogether!

We can use a website to store our bookmarks so that we can see them on any computer connected to the internet. You can do this on a website called Delicious.

### How to add a bookmark to Delicious

To add a bookmark to Delicious, look at the ribbon.

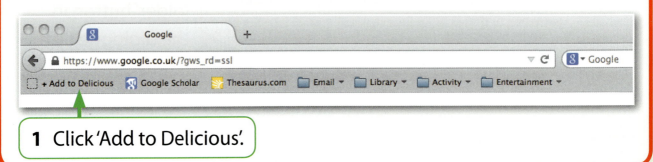

**1** Click 'Add to Delicious'.

**2** This is the URL.

**3** This is the page name.

A dialogue box will appear.

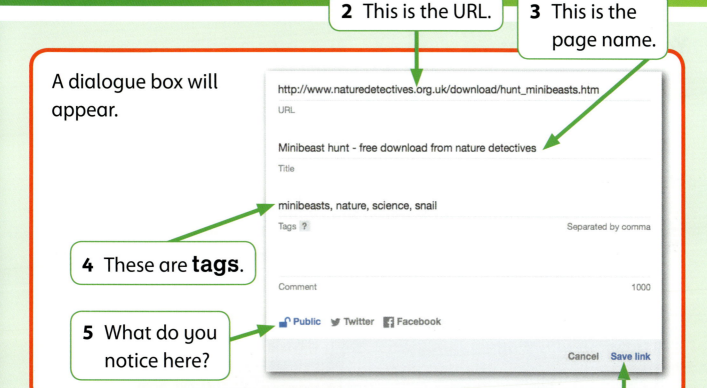

http://www.naturedetectives.org.uk/download/hunt_minibeasts.htm
URL

Minibeast hunt - free download from nature detectives
Title

minibeasts, nature, science, snail
Tags  ?                                          Separated by comma

Comment                                          1000

🔓 Public    🐦 Twitter    f Facebook

Cancel    **Save link**

**4** These are **tags**.

**5** What do you notice here?

**6** Click 'Save link'.

## Activity  Adding a bookmark to Delicious

Look at the website about snails.

Explore the website.

Add it to Delicious.

**If you have time…**

When you add a bookmark you can see a line of tags. What do you think a tag might be?

**Talk about…**

What did you like about the website on snails?

What did you not like?

Did you believe what you read?

Could you find what you needed?

43

## You will learn:

➜ about tags.

Nadine has been finding out about dragonflies.
She finds this information on a website:

Dragonflies are not dragons. They are insects. They have beautiful, shimmery wings and fly well. A dragonfly starts its life in water as a nymph. Then it sheds its skin and flies away.

Nadine wants to bookmark the website and tag important words. She has highlighted these.

## How to tag

Explore the page of a website carefully.

Choose the most important words.

Click 'Add to Delicious'.

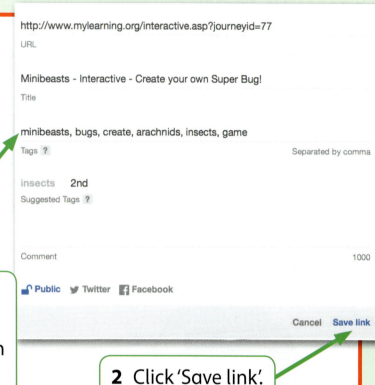

http://www.mylearning.org/interactive.asp?journeyid=77
URL

Minibeasts - Interactive - Create your own Super Bug!
Title

minibeasts, bugs, create, arachnids, insects, game
Tags ?                                    Separated by comma

insects    2nd
Suggested Tags ?

Comment                                              1000

🔓 Public    🐦 Twitter    f Facebook

Cancel   **Save link**

**1** This is the place for tags. Type in important words here. Put a comma between each word like this.

**2** Click 'Save link'.

## Activity  Tagging a website

Look at the website about dragonflies, shown on your screen.

Bookmark the pages you like by adding them to Delicious.

Add three tags then save the link.

## Talk about...

What tags would you look for if you were searching for websites about minibeasts?

## If you have time...

Compare your tags with another group. Were any tags the same?

## You will learn:

→ how to find links on a bookmarking site using a tag search.

Ali is looking for a website about ants.

He has tried a search engine, but there were too many choices.

He goes to Delicious. He will use other people's tags to find a good website.

### How to find websites using tags in Delicious

Press the 'Enter' key.

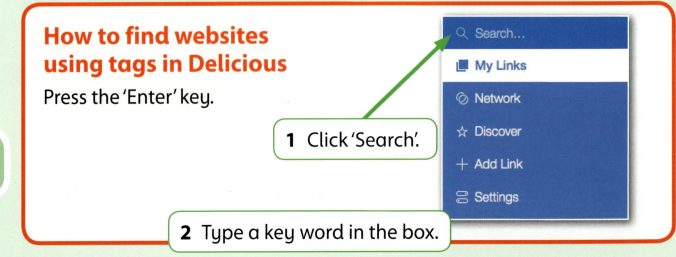

**1** Click 'Search'.

Q Search...

📖 My Links

⊘ Network

☆ Discover

+ Add Link

⊟ Settings

**2** Type a key word in the box.

Sometimes you will need more than one key word to find exactly what you need.

For example, searching for the tag 'ant' might give you lots of links you don't need. So you could search for 'ant habitat' for a better list.

## Activity  Using tags in Delicious

Type 'insect habitat' into the search box on Delicious.

→ What links do you find?

→ Which links look useful?

→ Which links are not useful, and why?

Show your teacher which link you would like to click.

Explore the site. If it is useful to you, add it to your favourites on Delicious. Don't forget to add some tags!

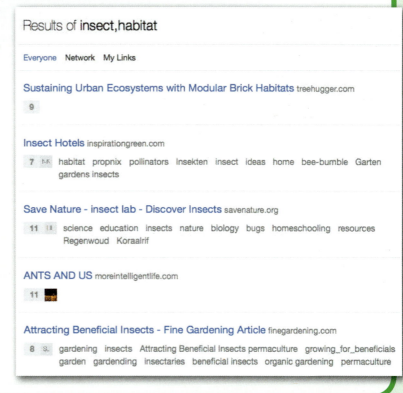

Results of **insect,habitat**

Everyone   Network   My Links

Sustaining Urban Ecosystems with Modular Brick Habitats treehugger.com
9

Insect Hotels inspirationgreen.com
7   KK   habitat  propnix  pollinators  Insekten  insect  ideas  home  bee-bumble  Garten  gardens  insects

Save Nature - insect lab - Discover Insects savenature.org
11   |||   science  education  insects  nature  biology  bugs  homeschooling  resources  Regenwoud  Koraalrif

ANTS AND US moreintelligentlife.com
11  ■

Attracting Beneficial Insects - Fine Gardening Article finegardening.com
8   S.   gardening  insects  Attracting Beneficial Insects  permaculture  growing_for_beneficials  garden  gardending  insectaries  beneficial insects  organic gardening  permaculture

## If you have time...

Type 'insect habitat' into a search engine. What sort of links do you see on the screen? Which do you think is more useful – Delicious or the search engine?

## You will learn:

→ to think carefully about what you see online.

What do you look at on a web page?

Do you look at the pictures to help you understand?

How do you choose where to go next?

When we are online, we are making choices all the time.

One of the choices we need to make is deciding whether the things we are reading online are true or false.

**Talk about...**
What kinds of books tell the truth?

### Activity | Checking websites

 Choose one of the links another group has bookmarked on Delicious.

Explore the site.

Fill in the worksheet your teacher gives you.

## How to check websites

When you are reading something online, ask yourself these questions:

**1** What do I want to find out?

**2** What did I look at first?

**3** What is the name of the site?

**4** Do I need to read every word very carefully?

**5** Does the site link to other safe sites?

**6** Are there pop-up adverts trying to sell me something?

**7** Who built the site?

### If you have time...

Your class has looked at, bookmarked and tagged some websites about minibeasts. Write about which sites have been the most interesting, and why.

# What you have learned about the internet

You have learned about search engines, bookmarking, tagging and being critical about what you see online.

The activities on this page will let you see how much you have learned.

1 Write instructions to tell someone how to bookmark a web page to Delicious.

_____

_____

_____

_____

_____

2 Write three questions to ask yourself when you visit a website.

_____

_____

_____

_____

_____

50

© Oxford University Press 2015

**3** Here is a picture of a web page. Fill in the labels on the worksheet your teacher gives you.

## Activity  Tagging a bookmark

Show your teacher how to tag a bookmark.

© Oxford University Press 2015

# 4 Handling data: Spreadsheet maths

**By the end of this unit you will:**

→ learn what a spreadsheet is

→ know how to use a spreadsheet to work out the answer to sums

→ learn why a spreadsheet makes sums easy to do.

**In this unit you are going to use a spreadsheet to do sums.**

A spreadsheet is a computer tool. It will work out the answers to sums. You will use a spreadsheet that has been made for you. Then you will make a spreadsheet of your own.

**Talk about...**

Look at your maths books for this year. Talk about the different maths topics you have studied. Which topics do you think a spreadsheet would be helpful for?

## Activity Maths challenge

Have a go at these maths questions.

Which ones were easy?

Which ones were hard?

🍎 + 🍎🍎🍎🍎 =

35 − 🍎🍎 =

10 − 🍎🍎🍎🍎🍎🍎🍎 =

cell    cell reference

formula    label

value    worksheet

▼ An accountant in a fruit packing factory using a ledger.

## Fascinating fact

Before computers were invented, accountants used ledgers (books of pages with carefully arranged lines) to work out money spent and money earned.

Computer spreadsheets look similar to ledgers, but the computer works out the sums.

## You will learn:

→ the layout of a spreadsheet
→ how to change the values in a spreadsheet.

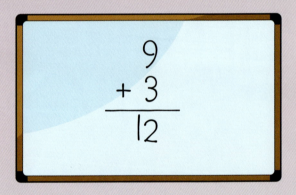

A spreadsheet has been made for you to use. Your teacher will show you how to open the spreadsheet.

You will see the spreadsheet on your screen. It shows an addition sum like the sum on this whiteboard.

$$\begin{array}{r} 9 \\ + 3 \\ \hline 12 \end{array}$$

The spreadsheet is made of columns and rows. Each column has a letter. Each row has a number.

Where a column crosses a row, this makes a **cell**.

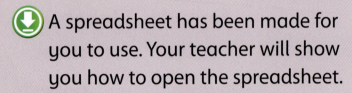

This cell has letters in it. This is called a **label**.

This cell has numbers in it. This is called a **value**.

## How to change the contents of a cell

1  Move the mouse cursor to the cell.

2  Click the mouse button to select the cell.

3  Type the new value or label.

4  Press the 'Enter' key.

The number 9 is in cell B3.

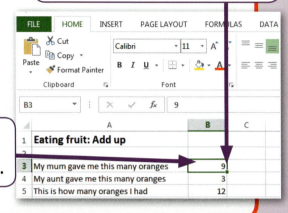

Cell B3 is selected. This cell is called B3 because it is where row 3 crosses column B.

## Activity  Entering new values

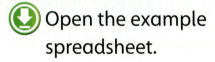

Open the example spreadsheet.

Click on cell B3. Type the number 7. Press the 'Enter' key.

Click on cell B4. Type the number 10. Press the 'Enter' key.

Save your work in your own storage area.

The answer to the addition sum is shown here.

**If you have time…**

Try entering different numbers in cells B3 and B4. See the results of these changes.

## You will learn:

→ what a worksheet is
→ how to select different worksheets.

The grid that you see on the screen is called a **worksheet**. A spreadsheet file can have more than one worksheet.

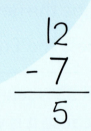

$$\begin{array}{r} 12 \\ -\ 7 \\ \hline 5 \end{array}$$

| | A | B |
|---|---|---|
| 1 | **Eating fruit: Add up** | |
| 2 | | |
| 3 | My mum gave me this many oranges | 9 |
| 4 | My aunt gave me this many oranges | 3 |
| 5 | This is how many oranges I had | 12 |
| | ◄ ► **Add** Take away Times Sharing | |

These four tabs show that this spreadsheet file has four worksheets.

### How to see the worksheets

⬇ Open your saved spreadsheet file. To see the different worksheets, click on the different tabs.

**1** Click on the tab 'Take away'.

| | A | B | C |
|---|---|---|---|
| 1 | **Eating fruit: Take away** | | |
| 2 | | | |
| 3 | I had this many grapes | 12 | |
| 4 | I ate this many grapes | 7 | |
| 5 | This is how many grapes I had left | 5 | |
| | ◄ ► Add **Take away** Times Sharing | | |

**2** This spread shows a take away problem. You start with 12 grapes, you eat 7.

**3** You have 5 grapes left.

## Activity [Taking away]

Select the 'Take away' worksheet. Use the spreadsheet to do a take away calculation.

| | A | B |
|---|---|---|
| 1 | **Eating fruit: Take away** | |
| 2 | | |
| 3 | I had this many grapes | 99 |
| 4 | I ate this many grapes | 71 |
| 5 | This is how many grapes I had left | 28 |
| 6 | | |
| 7 | | |
| 8 | | |

**1** Change the number of grapes you start with. Press the 'Enter' key.

**2** Change the number of grapes you eat. Press the 'Enter' key.

**3** See how the final value has changed.

 **If you have time...**

Look at the other worksheets in this spreadsheet file. Make changes to the values on those worksheets and see what happens.

**Talk about...**

Have you used a calculator? How is a spreadsheet different from using a calculator?

## You will learn:

→ what cell references are
→ how cell references are used in formulas
→ the signs used in formulas.

### 💭 Remember

Every cell in a worksheet has a name.
The name is made of the column letter and the row number.
This name is called the **cell reference**.

> **3** The cell content is shown here.

Look at the 'Times' worksheet.
It shows a multiplication problem.

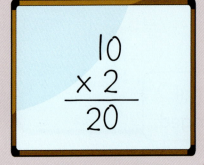

| B3 | ▼ | : | ✕ | ✓ | $f_x$ | 2 |

| | A | B | C |
|---|---|---|---|
| 1 | **Eating fruit: Times** | | |
| 2 | | | |
| 3 | Every pupil in my class gave the teacher | 2 | apples |
| 4 | How many pupils in the class | 10 | |
| 5 | How many apples for my teacher | 20 | |

> **2** The cell reference is shown here.

> **1** This cell is selected.

You have learned that spreadsheet cells contain values and labels.

> **2** The cell content is shown here. It is a formula.

Some spreadsheet cells contain **formulas**.
Formulas work out the answers to calculations.
Every formula begins with an equals sign.

| B5 | ▼ | : | ✕ | ✓ | $f_x$ | =B3*B4 |

| | A | B | C |
|---|---|---|---|
| 1 | **Eating fruit: Times** | | |
| 2 | | | |
| 3 | Every pupil in my class gave the teacher | 2 | apples |
| 4 | How many pupils in the class | 10 | |
| 5 | How many apples for my teacher | 20 | |
| 6 | | | |
| 7 | | | |

> **1** This cell is selected.

## How to understand formulas

The formula says:

$$= B3 * B4$$

\* stands for **times** (multiply)

So the formula says:

The number in cell B3 **times** the number in cell B4.

## Talk about...

There are four signs used by formulas. They are:

| + | – | * | / |

What do these four signs stand for?

## Activity  Finding formulas

Look at all the worksheets. Write down all the formulas you can find.

Next to each formula write down in words what you think the formula says.

## You will learn:

→ how spreadsheets show division
→ about decimals and fractions.

On the 'Sharing' tab you will see a division problem. Eighteen mangoes are shared among six friends – how many does each get?

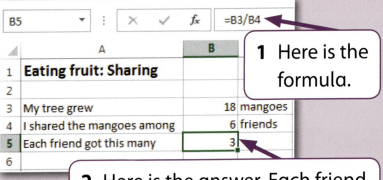

**1** Here is the formula.

**2** Here is the answer. Each friend gets three mangoes.

$$18 \div 6 = 3$$

### How to share (fractions and decimals)

If you change the values in the spreadsheet, the answer will change. Not all the answers will be a whole number – some will be part of a whole. If two mangoes are shared between four friends, each friend will have half (½) a mango. Half is a fraction.

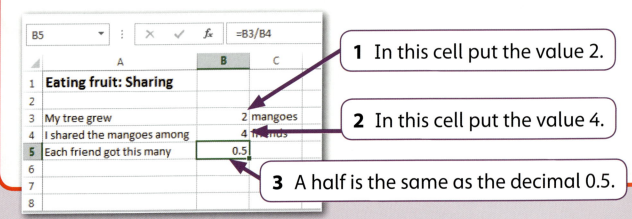

**1** In this cell put the value 2.

**2** In this cell put the value 4.

**3** A half is the same as the decimal 0.5.

## Activity  Sharing

 Change the values in the spreadsheet to see the result.

Try these values. Write down the problem and the answer you get.

➜  3 mangoes shared among 6 friends

➜  2 mangoes shared among 8 friends

➜  6 mangoes shared among 4 friends.

## Talk about...

Every fraction has a matching decimal. Here are some examples:

| One quarter | = | $\frac{1}{4}$ | = 0.25 |
|---|---|---|---|
| One half | = | $\frac{1}{2}$ | = 0.5 |
| Three quarters | = | $\frac{3}{4}$ | = 0.75 |
| One and a half | = | $1\frac{1}{2}$ | = 1.5 |

What other fractions have you learned about?

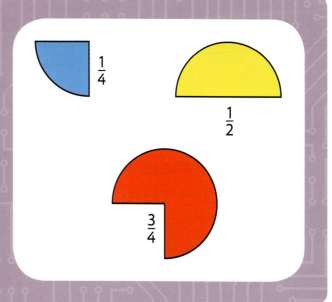

$\frac{1}{4}$

$\frac{1}{2}$

$\frac{3}{4}$

## You will learn:

→ how to enter values and labels into a spreadsheet
→ how to create a new spreadsheet.

### How to enter labels on a new spreadsheet

⬇ Start with a new blank spreadsheet file. You are going to add labels to this spreadsheet.

If a label is too big for a cell, it spills over into the space that follows.

**1** Select cell A1 and type 'Collecting shells'. Press the 'Enter' key.

**2** Select cell A3 and type 'my sister collected this many shells'. Press the 'Enter' key.

**3** Add this label to cell A4. Press the 'Enter' key.

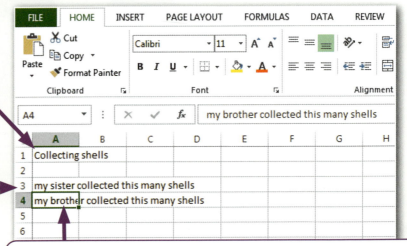

**1** Enter 5 in this cell.

### How to enter values

When values are typed into a cell, they move to the right of the cell. When text does this it is called right-justified. What do you think left-justified means?

**2** Enter 7 in this cell.

## Activity   Creating a spreadsheet

Create the spreadsheet about collecting shells by entering labels and values into the cells.

 Save your work.

## If you have time…

You have learned how to format text. Spreadsheet software gives you the same format options.

Change the formatting of the cells in your spreadsheet. You can choose any format you like.

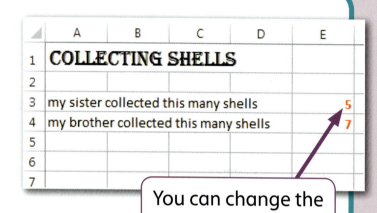

| | A | B | C | D | E |
|---|---|---|---|---|---|
| 1 | COLLECTING SHELLS | | | | |
| 2 | | | | | |
| 3 | my sister collected this many shells | | | | 5 |
| 4 | my brother collected this many shells | | | | 7 |
| 5 | | | | | |
| 6 | | | | | |
| 7 | | | | | |

You can change the colour of the font.

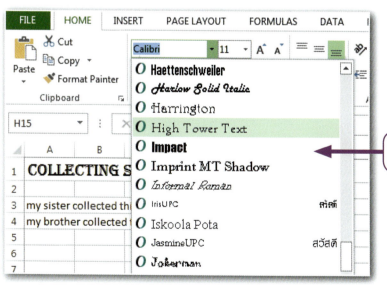

You can change the font.

## Talk about…

Why do spreadsheets have labels as well as values? Labels are not used in formulas – so why are they useful?

## You will learn:

→ how to use a spreadsheet formula to work out a result.

This is a spreadsheet made by a student. Like you, this student has entered labels and values.

This student has also entered a formula to work out the total number of shells.

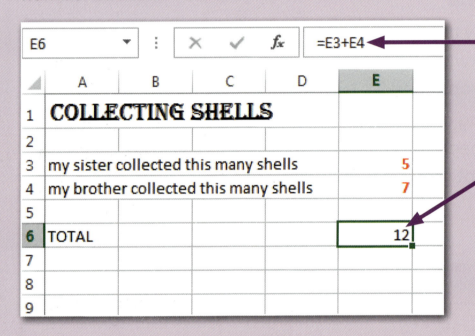

**1** Here is the formula the student entered.

**2** Here is the result of the formula.

**2** Type an equals sign here.

## How to start a formula

First, you must enter a label. Select cell A6. Type 'TOTAL' and press the 'Enter' key.

Next, you must enter the formula. Every formula starts with an equals sign.

**1** Type 'TOTAL' here.

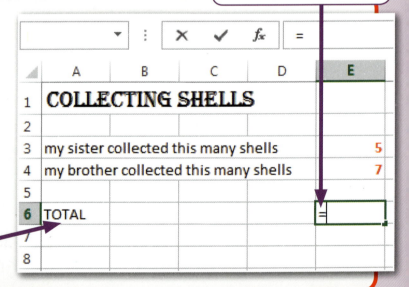

# How to build a formula

To build a formula you add cell references.

 **Remember**

To add a cell reference to a formula, you must click on that cell.

Press the 'Enter' key when the formula is complete.

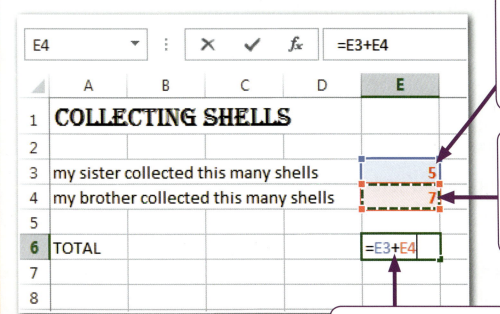

**1** Click on cell E3, and E3 will be added to the formula.

**3** Click on cell E4, and E4 will be added to the formula.

**2** Type the plus sign in the formula.

---

**Activity** Building a formula

 Enter the 'TOTAL' label.

Enter a formula to work out the total number of shells.

---

**If you have time...**

Make a bigger spreadsheet which adds up the shells collected by four different people. Enter labels, values and a formula.

# What you have learned about handling data

You have learned how to use spreadsheets to work out the answers to maths problems.

The activities on this page will let you see how much you have learned.

**1** What are the small squares in a worksheet called?

_____

**2** What is a worksheet?

_____

**3** What do the labels in a spreadsheet do?

_____

**4** A cell reference has one letter and one number. What do the letter and number tell you?

_____

**5** What sign comes at the start of a spreadsheet formula?

_____

**6** What does this sign (*) mean?

_____

**7** How do you add a cell reference to a formula?

_____

© Oxford University Press 2015

## Activity: Labelling a spreadsheet

⬇ Your teacher will give you a resource sheet that shows this spreadsheet. Add labels to show:

→ a label

→ a value

→ a formula

→ the result of a formula.

| D7 | ▼ | : | ✕ | ✓ | *fx* | =D3+D4+D5 |
|---|---|---|---|---|---|---|

| | A | B | C | D | E |
|---|---|---|---|---|---|
| 1 | Catching fish | | | | |
| 2 | | | | | |
| 3 | Ali catches this many fish | | | 44 | |
| 4 | Reza catches this many fish | | | 29 | |
| 5 | Khadija catches this many fish | | | 36 | |
| 6 | | | | | |
| 7 | TOTAL FISH | | | 109 | |
| 8 | | | | | |
| 9 | | | | | |

## Activity: Writing a spreadsheet formula

⬇ Here is a spreadsheet that works out how many cookies you have left. Use the skills you have learned to make this spreadsheet. Enter the formula that will work out the result.

| D6 | ▼ | : | ✕ | ✓ | *fx* | =D3-D4 |
|---|---|---|---|---|---|---|

| | A | B | C | D | E |
|---|---|---|---|---|---|
| 1 | Friends and cookies | | | | |
| 2 | | | | | |
| 3 | I had this many cookies | | | 9 | |
| 4 | I gave this many to my friend | | | 4 | |
| 5 | | | | | |
| 6 | I had this many left | | | 5 | |
| 7 | | | | | |

© Oxford University Press 2015

# 5 Computers in society: Technology at work

**By the end of this unit you will:**

→ understand how different people use technology

→ learn to ask someone questions about how they use technology in a polite way

→ know how to share a piece of equipment

→ understand how to share what you found with others.

In this unit you are going to find out how people use **technology** to help them in their work.

We all use technology to help us do everyday things. We use technology when we phone a friend, go on the computer or put washing in the washing machine.

## Activity | Finding technologies

Look at the technologies in the picture. Take photos, draw or cut out pictures from catalogues to show as many different technologies as you can.

interview    problem

question    recording

technician    technology

## Fascinating fact

Most people blink their eyes around 20 times per minute, while a computer user only blinks around 7 times per minute. Blink!

## You will learn:

→ how we use technology in everyday life.

Here are some people who use technology in their daily lives. They are using technology to solve **problems**.

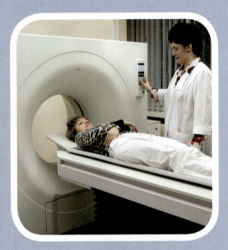

▲ doctor

▲ teacher

▲ engineer

## How do people use technology at work?

People use technology in different ways at home…

for living

for transport

to communicate

for fun

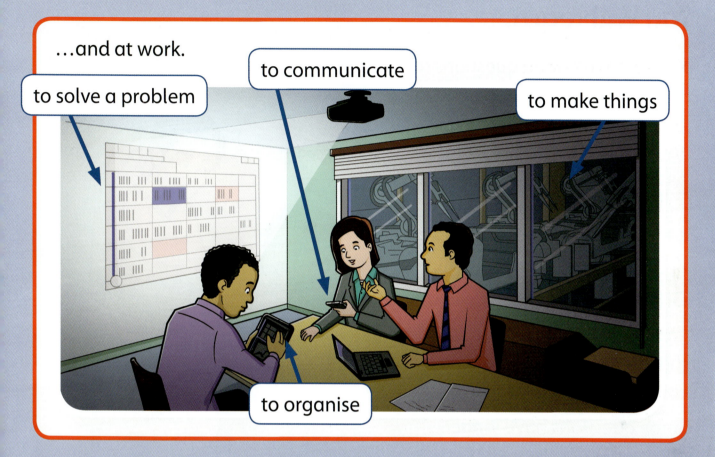

…and at work.

to communicate

to solve a problem

to make things

to organise

## Activity   Looking at technology in the workplace

 Look at the worksheet your teacher has given you. Carry out the activity.

How is technology helping these people?

### Talk about…
What kinds of technology do you think are used most often? Why?

### If you have time…

What do you think these people would have used before digital technologies?

➔ a doctor

➔ a teacher

➔ an office worker

5 Computers in society: Technology at work

71

## You will learn:

→ how to ask good questions about the ways people use technology.

You can find out about how people use technology for their work by asking **questions**. You need to think of good questions to get useful answers.

### Different kinds of questions

Some questions have answers that are 'yes' or 'no'. These are called 'closed' questions.

Some questions have longer answers. These are called 'open' questions.

Open questions start with:

→ Who

→ What

→ When

→ Where

→ Why

Do you like to read?

Yes.

How does technology help you?

It helps me in lots of ways. It...

### How to write questions

⬇ Look at the worksheet your teacher will give you. Work out which are closed questions and which are open questions.

## Talk about...

What questions might you ask someone about the technology they use?

Think about:

→ their day

→ when they might use technology

→ how they might use technology.

## Activity  Writing questions

Work in a small group.

Write five questions.

Think about who you will be speaking to.

What questions can you ask them about how they use technology?

## If you have time...

Your teacher will show you a short news clip. What do you notice about:

→ the equipment that is being used

→ the way the people stand or sit

→ the kinds of questions being asked?

Practise asking and answering some questions with a partner. Do you feel comfortable being asked questions? What would make you feel more comfortable?

## You will learn:

➜ how to share technology
➜ how to ask questions politely.

During this lesson we are going to ask a visitor our questions. This is called an **interview**. You are the 'interviewers'. The visitor is the 'interviewee'. It is important to be polite to the interviewee.

Your group will be able to record your interview. You will use these **recordings** in your next lesson.

interviewee

interviewer

## Talk about...

What recording devices could you use? Why is it important to share technology?

# How to record your interview

**1** Look at the questions you wrote last week.

**2** Decide who is going to ask which question.

**3** Write your name next to your question.

**4** Agree who is going to work the recorder.

💭 Remember

➔ to greet your visitor politely

➔ to ask your visitor permission to record the interview

➔ to thank them at the end.

Please may we record your interview? We will not share it with anyone. It will only be for us to use after this interview.

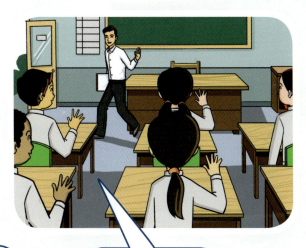

Thank you for your time.

## Activity  Interviewing

Carry out your interview.

### If you have time…

Think about how you might show others what you have found out.

## You will learn:

→ about listening to recordings
→ about how people use technology.

When people do a recording of an interview, they listen to it afterwards and take notes. You are going to do the same with the recording you made of a visitor telling you about how they use technology.

This is a professional recording studio where music and interviews are recorded. The **technicians** listen and edit the recordings to make them sound good. They use computers and technological devices to do this.

# How to listen carefully

In pairs or groups listen to your recording and note down the most important things that were said in the interview. This is how you do it.

**2** These students are listening to the recording and telling the technician when to stop and start.

**1** This is the technician – they stop and start the recording.

**3** The students take notes of anything interesting they hear.

## Activity  Listening to the recording

Listen and take notes of your recording.

## Talk about...
What kinds of questions got the best answers?

What technology was used most often?

What technology was used least often?

## If you have time...
Look at the magazine article your teacher has given you. Make a list of the important words in the article. Why are these words important?

## You will learn:

➜ how to share your findings in a poster presentation.

You have interviewed a visitor about the ways they use technology.

You have listened to your interview and written down the important things your visitor said.

Now you are going to give a presentation to share with the rest of the class about what you found out.

**Talk about...**
Why is it important to share information?

### How to give a presentation

Sales people give presentations to sell their products.

Teachers give presentations when they take a lesson.

They often use pictures and diagrams to make the presentation more interesting. Images also help to explain what you want to say.

For your presentation you could draw a poster with the information you found out about in your interview.

## Activity  Preparing your presentation

Plan your presentation. Decide who is going to talk and what they are going to say. Prepare a poster to go with your presentation.

## Talk about...

People use technology in presentations. What technology is this person using?

## If you have time...

Practise your presentation.

## You will learn:

➜ how to share information.

You have interviewed a visitor and found out what technologies they use to solve problems.

In this lesson you are going to share what you have found with the whole class.

**3** Make eye contact. That means try to look at the people you are speaking to.

## How to share what you have found out

When you give a presentation it is important that everyone can hear and see you.

Here are some tips to help you.

**1** Stand up tall. Pretend you have a piece of string coming out of the top of your head, pulling you up straight like a puppet.

**2** Speak slowly and clearly. Try to take good deep breaths in and out.

### Activity | Sharing

Take turns to share what you found out about the technologies your visitor used. You could tell the whole class or a smaller group.

### Activity | Technology in the future

⬇ Complete the sentence on the worksheet your teacher gives you. What technology do you think you might be using in the future?

 **If you have time...**

Write a top tips list for giving a presentation.

### Talk about...

What did you find out about technology at work?

What problems did technology solve?

What made your presentation go well?

What could be done to make it even better?

# What you have learned about computers in society

You have learned how people use technology; how to ask questions politely; how to share a piece of equipment and how to share information with others.

The activities on this page will let you see how much you have learned.

**1** Write down five types of technology.

_____

_____

**2** Look at these pictures.

**a** Write down the names of these technologies.

_____

**b** What kinds of problems do each of these technologies solve?

_____

_____

© Oxford University Press 2015

**3** Why did you have to share recording equipment?

_____

_____

_____

**4** What was difficult about sharing equipment?

_____

_____

_____

**5** What was fun about sharing equipment?

_____

_____

_____

**Activity** | **Interviewing about technologies**

Ask another student questions about which technologies they like using and why.

© Oxford University Press 2015

# 6 Control the computer: The lively cat

**By the end of this unit you will:**

→ understand what computer programs are

→ know how to open and run a computer program

→ know how to make changes to a computer program.

In this unit you will control a cat that walks and talks on the computer screen.

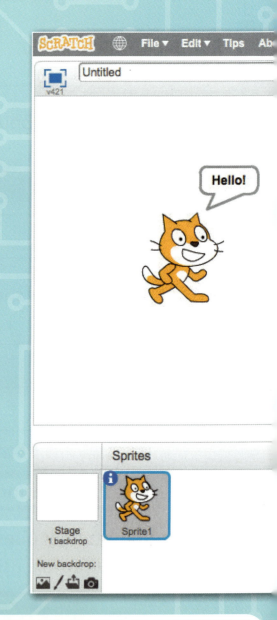

A **computer program** is a set of instructions. The instructions control what the computer does. In this unit you will learn how to make changes to a computer program that will change what the computer does.

**Talk about...**
What computer games do you know?
Which games are your favourites?

## Activity  Drawing an animal

Look at the picture. It shows the cat that walks and talks on the computer screen. Think of a different animal you would like to see. Draw the animal.

programming language

stage

block          script

computer program

backdrop

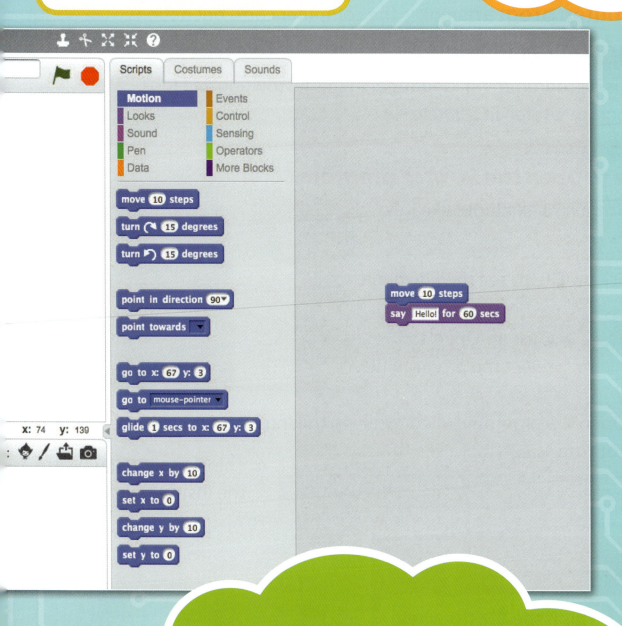

## Fascinating fact

*Scratch* is used in schools all over the world. There are schools in more than 150 different countries that use *Scratch*.

## You will learn:

➔ what *Scratch* is
➔ how to run a *Scratch* program.

A **computer program** makes the computer carry out actions.

A **programming language** is used to write computer programs.

*Scratch* is a programming language. In this lesson you will look at a program written in *Scratch*.

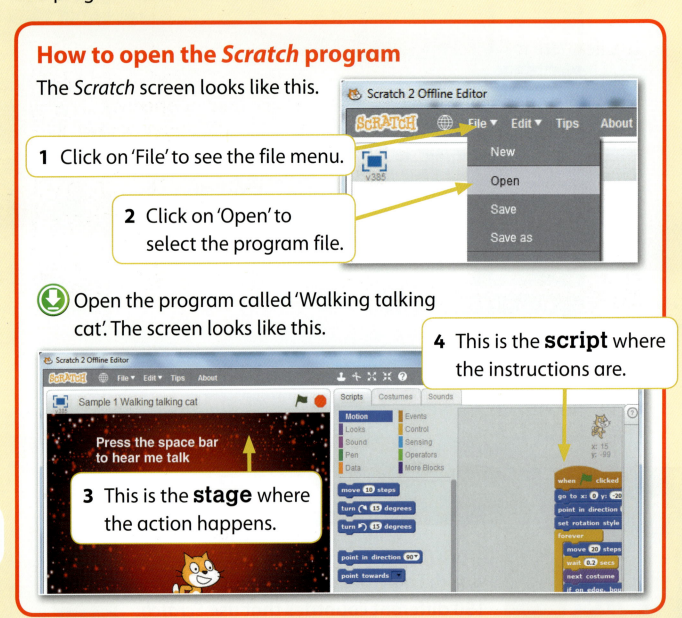

### How to open the *Scratch* program

The *Scratch* screen looks like this.

**1** Click on 'File' to see the file menu.

**2** Click on 'Open' to select the program file.

Open the program called 'Walking talking cat'. The screen looks like this.

**4** This is the **script** where the instructions are.

Press the space bar to hear me talk

**3** This is the **stage** where the action happens.

## Activity — Running the *Scratch* program

Run the *Scratch* program.

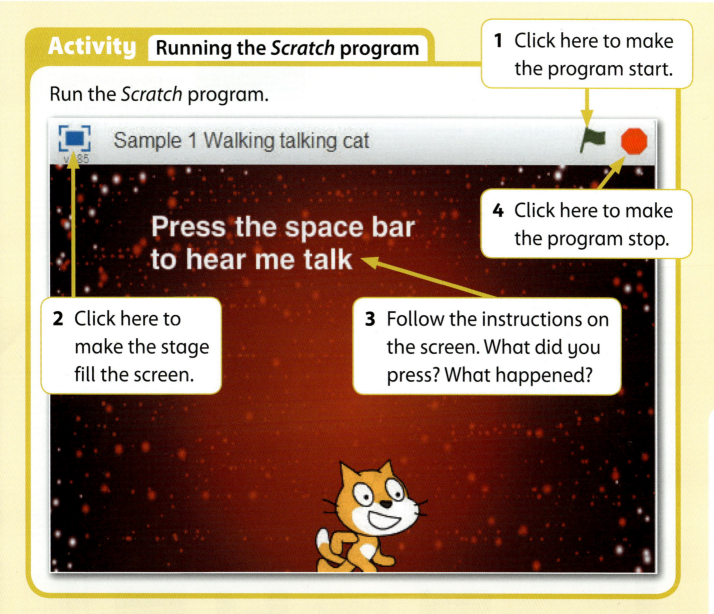

**1** Click here to make the program start.

Sample 1 Walking talking cat

v 85

Press the space bar to hear me talk

**4** Click here to make the program stop.

**2** Click here to make the stage fill the screen.

**3** Follow the instructions on the screen. What did you press? What happened?

## Talk about...
What new words have you learned?

## If you have time...
Click on the screen size icon. This will make the stage smaller.
Look at the 'Script' side of the screen. Can you work out what these instructions do?

## You will learn:

→ what the backdrop is
→ how to choose a backdrop for the *Scratch* program.

This screen has a bright red **backdrop**. The backdrop is the image that fills up the background. Now you will choose a new backdrop from the library. A library is a collection of resources.

**1** Below the stage you can see the backdrop.

**2** Click here to open the backdrop library.

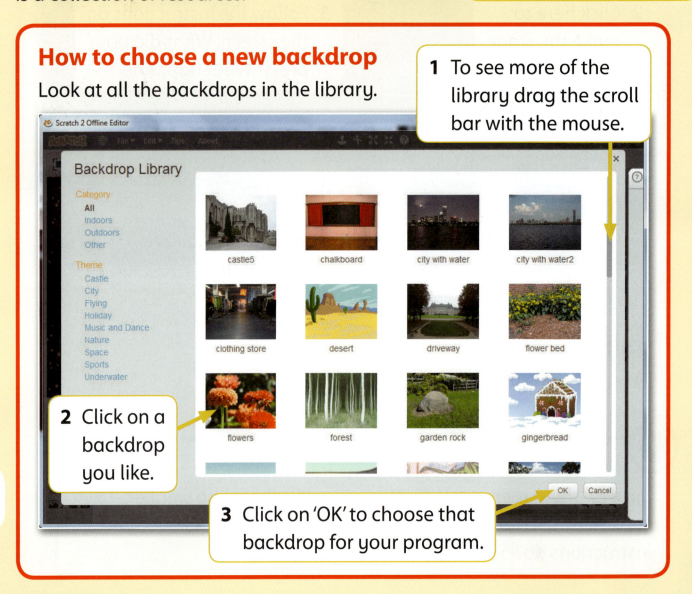

### How to choose a new backdrop

Look at all the backdrops in the library.

**1** To see more of the library drag the scroll bar with the mouse.

**2** Click on a backdrop you like.

**3** Click on 'OK' to choose that backdrop for your program.

## Activity | Choosing a backdrop

🔽 Choose your backdrop for your program.

Save your program when you have finished.

 **If you have time...**

You can use any image as a backdrop. You can use an image stored on your computer. You can use a photo on your camera. Don't forget to connect your camera to the computer to download your photo.

**1** Click here to choose an image from the computer.

**2** Click here to take an image from your camera.

## Talk about...

What background did you choose? Why did you pick that one? What did you like about it?

## You will learn:

→ how sounds are included in a *Scratch* program
→ how to choose new sounds for a *Scratch* program.

Open your saved program. It might look like this. You chose a new background. Now you are going to choose new sounds. They are in a sound library.

**1** Click here to work with sound.

**2** Click here to open the sound library.

## How to choose sounds from the sound library

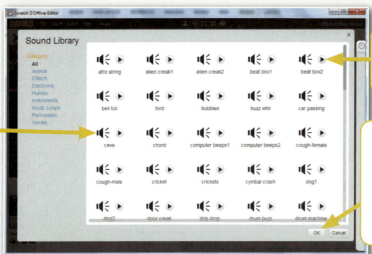

**2** Click on any sound to select it.

**1** Click to listen to any sound.

**3** Click on 'OK' to choose that sound for your program.

## Talk about...

What might be the best sounds for a cat?

## Activity  Choosing sounds

 Choose three or more sounds to add to the *Scratch* program.

Save your work.

Next lesson you will learn how to make the cat say the new sounds you have added.

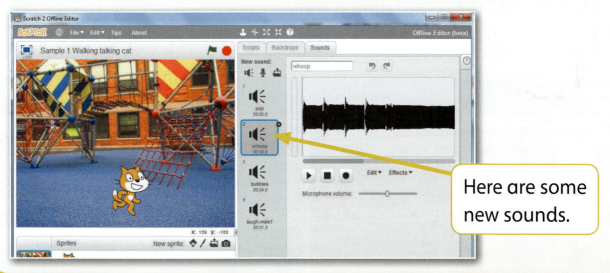

Here are some new sounds.

## If you have time...

There are more ways to get sounds. Add new sounds to the program using one of these ways.

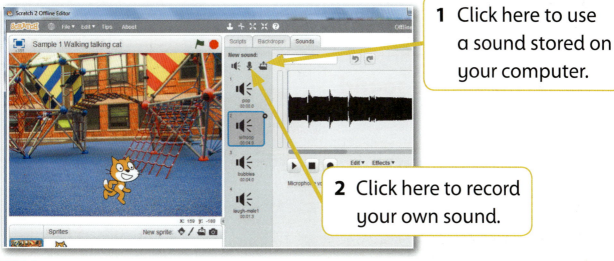

**1** Click here to use a sound stored on your computer.

**2** Click here to record your own sound.

## You will learn:

→ how to edit a *Scratch* program
→ how to change the sounds used in a *Scratch* program.

Open your saved program. Look at the script. The script tells the computer what to do. Now you will change the script.

• You will change the sound the cat makes.

• You will change the words on the screen.

**1** This script will run when you press the space bar.

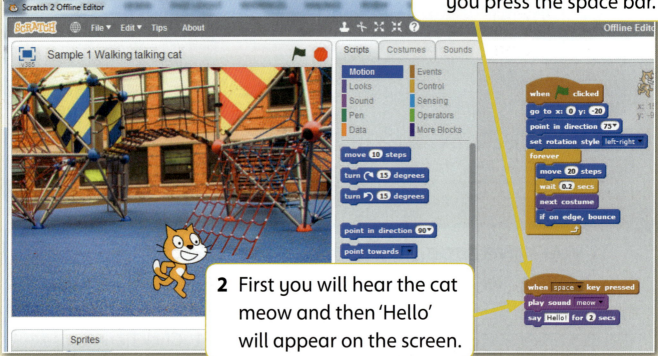

**2** First you will hear the cat meow and then 'Hello' will appear on the screen.

**How to change the sound**

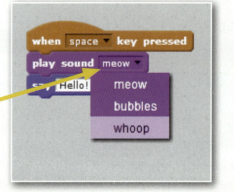

Click here to choose a new sound from your list.

## How to change the word

Type a new word. The cat will say that word.

**1** Type a new word here.

You can change the keyboard key that makes the cat speak.

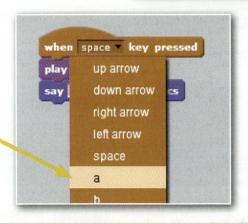

**2** Click on a key from this list.

**Talk about...**

What word might the cat say?

## Activity   Changing sounds

 Change the cat's sound. Change the word the cat says.

Run your script. Do you like the change you made?

Save your file.

**2** Choose what key you press to run the new script.

## If you have time...

You can make two scripts. Change the key press, the sound and the words for the new script.

**1** Click the right button on the mouse. Choose 'duplicate' to make a new script.

## You will learn:

➜ how a *Scratch* script controls movement
➜ how to change the movement of a sprite.

The cat is a 'sprite'. A sprite is an object controlled by a computer program.

Look on the right of the *Scratch* screen. You will see the script. In this lesson you will change the script.

The script is made up of **blocks**. You can add new blocks to the script.

**1** This is the script.

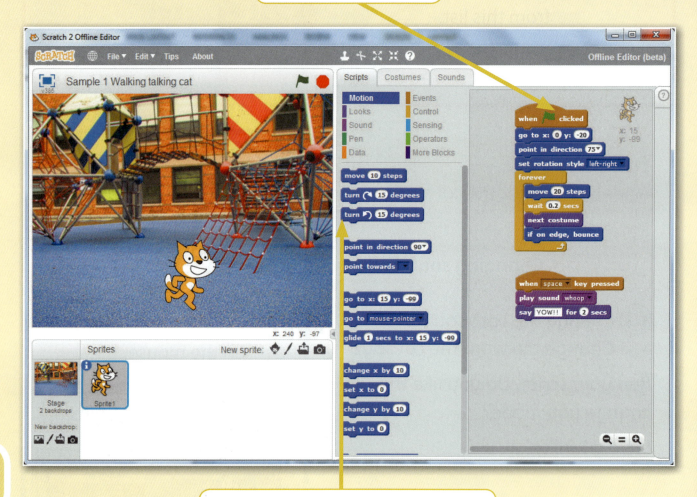

**2** These are spare blocks which you can add to the script.

# How to make the cat move

You are going to make the cat turn.

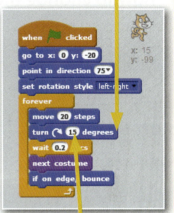

**2** Add the block to the script here.

**1** Click and drag this block to the script.

**3** You can type a different number.

## Activity  Turning

 Add the 'turn' block to the script.

What happens when you run the script?

Save your work.

The number in the 'turn' block shows how much the cat will turn.
The bigger the number, the more the cat will turn.

## Talk about...
Turning is described in degrees. 360 degrees is one full circle. What is half a circle?

## If you have time...
Change the number in the 'turn' block. What happens to the cat?

Try different numbers. See what happens.

## You will learn:

→ how to make *Scratch* draw with a pen
→ how to change the pen colour and size.

Open the *Scratch* file called 'The drawing bug 1'. Find the stage and the script.

Start the program. The bug is ready to draw. Have a go. Draw a line.

Now you will make changes to the program.

### How to change the line that you draw

Every colour has a number – red is number 0, yellow is 30 and green is 60.

**1** You can change the colour of the line by changing this number.

**2** You can change the size of the pen here – 1 is a thin line, 30 is a fat line.

## Activity   Changing the colour and size of the pen

Change the colour and size of the pen.

Run the program. Draw a line on the screen.

Save your work.

## How to make the pen colour change

You can add a new block to the script. It will make the pen colour change while you are drawing.

**1** Click here to see the blocks that change the pen.

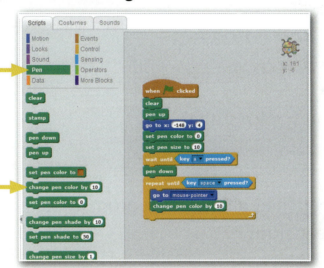

**2** Click and drag this block to the script.

## If you have time...

Add the 'change pen colour' block to the script. Now you can draw a rainbow line.

## Talk about...
Do you like to draw with one colour or with rainbow colours?

# What you have learned about controlling the computer

You have learned about a computer program. You have edited a program to make it work in different ways. You have changed the images and sounds used by the program and made a sprite move.

The activities on this page will let you see how much you have learned.

**1** What is a *Scratch* sprite?

_____

**2** What is a *Scratch* script?

_____

**3** What is the *Scratch* stage?

_____

**4** You have opened a *Scratch* program. What happens when you click on the green flag?

_____

**5** You are running a *Scratch* program. What happens when you click on the big red dot?

_____

**6** Describe two ways you can make changes to a *Scratch* program.

_____

_____

© Oxford University Press 2015

## Activity | Knowing about *Scratch* features

**1** Which parts of this picture represent:

➔ the stage

➔ the script

➔ the sprite?

**2** What other features do you recognise on this screen?

## Activity | Changing the backdrop

Open 'The drawing bug 2' program file.

Change the backdrop to a picture of flowers.

Save your work.

## Activity | Changing the sound

Load the sound called 'xylo 1' from the sound library.

**1** Drag the 'play sound' block here.

Run the script. What happens?

**2** Click on the 'play sound' block and change it to 'xylo 1'.

© Oxford University Press 2015

# Glossary

**backdrop**  the image in the background of the *Scratch* stage

**backspace**  the key that makes the cursor move backwards, erasing the previous word

**block**  the small sections of a *Scratch* program that fit to together to make the program code

**bookmark**  a way of recording a website address

**brochure**  a small booklet that has words and pictures to tell you about something

**browser**  a program that helps you look at pages on websites

**cell**  a square on the spreadsheet grid

**cell reference**  the name of a cell in the spreadsheet grid, formed by combining the column letter and the row number

**Clip Art** small pictures you can use in your work

**computer program** a set of stored instructions which control how the computer works

**cursor** a movable image, often an arrow or pointing hand, on a computer screen showing the point that will be affected by an action from the user

**delete** to remove something from your screen

**document** a piece of writing that can be printed on paper, or electronic

**edit** to add to, remove, correct or change something to make it better

**effects** changes you can make to your pictures to make them look nicer

**favourite** a way of recording a website address

**formula** instructions for the spreadsheet to calculate a value

**internet** a network of computers that goes across the whole world

# Glossary

**interview** asking questions to find out answers

**keyboard** the part of the computer used to type letters

**label** text entered into a spreadsheet cell

**library** a collection of digital resources

**line break** to start a new line of writing

**page elements** the parts of a page layout, like words, pictures and titles

**problem** something that needs to be fixed

**programming language** a language used to write computer programs

**question** a sentence that needs an answer

**recording**  to copy sounds onto a machine so that they can be heard again

**Scratch**  a programming language designed for use by young learners

**screen**  the part of the computer where you see your work

**script**  a program written in *Scratch*

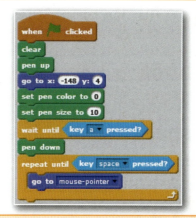

**search engine**  a program that collects information about websites so that you can find them easily

**stage**  an area of the screen where a *Scratch* script

**tag**  a key word

**technician**  a person who specialises in a type of technology (for example, audio technician, computer technician)

# Glossary

**technology**  any machine or device we can use to solve a problem

**template**  an outline that helps you make up a page. It shows your where to put your words and pictures

**URL**  the address of a website – URL stands for 'Uniform Resource Locator'

**value**  a number in a spreadsheet; can be used in calculations

**workbook**  a collection of spreadsheet grids in one file

**worksheet**  a spreadsheet grid which can hold labels, values and formulas

**Word Art** A way of making your words look more colourful or shaped